Joyous
Journey

Life is a journey, not a home
A road, not a city of habitation.
And its enjoyment and blessings
We have are inns on the roadside
    of life,
Where we may be refreshed for a
    moment
That we may with new strength
    press on to its end
To the rest that remains for the
    people of God.

—Lola R. Carr

Joyous Journey

CLINTON T. HOWELL

THOMAS NELSON INC., PUBLISHERS

Nashville   •   New York

Acknowledgement

It is the editor's belief that the necessary permissions from authors of the selections herein or their authorized agents have been obtained. In the event of any question arising as to the use of any selection, the editor, while expressing regret for any error he unconsciously made, will be pleased to make the necessary arrangement and correction in future editions of this book.

The editor has also made every effort to trace the authorship of all selections. When no name appears the authorship is unknown.

Chosen from among the great works of the English wood engraver Thomas Bewick (1753-1828), the delightful illustrations lend a distinct atmosphere to the book. Bewick is credited with the revival—and survival—of wood engraving as an art, bringing it back from the low degree to which it had fallen since the sixteenth century.

Library of Congress Cataloging in Publication Data
Main entry under title:

Joyous journey.

1. Quotations, English.   I. Howell, Clinton Talmadge, 1913—
PN6081.J65   828'.02   78-14341
ISBN 0-8407-5137-0

Preface

The selected poems and talks in this volume have been called the "literature of power" in their strength to guide, encourage, and inspire people in the battle for successful living.

> We are all but fellow travelers
> Along life's weary way;
> If any man can play the pipes,
> In God's name let him play!

> *—John Bennett*

"It is better to inspire the heart with a noble sentiment than to teach the mind a truth of science," said Edward Brooks.

The pilgrimage, in quest of gathering these spiritual provisions, has been exciting and joy-filled. The search through ancient and contemporary poetry, through the golden volumes of classical and contemporary writing, has been, indeed, a labor of love.

Clinton T. Howell

ASPIRATION

From "The Three Best Things"

Let me but live my life from year to year,
  With forward face and unreluctant soul;
  Not hurrying to, nor turning from, the goal;
Not mourning for the things that disappear
In the dim past, nor holding back in fear
  From what the future veils; but with a whole
  And happy heart that pays its toll
To Youth and Age, and travels on with cheer.

So let the way wind up the hill or down,
  O'er rough or smooth, the journey will be joy:
  Still seeking what I sought when but a boy,
New friendship, high adventure, and a crown,
  My heart will keep the courage of the quest,
  And hope the road's last turn will be the best.

—*Henry Van Dyke*

This Pilgrim Journey

"Few and evil have been the days of the years of my pilgrimage," said Jacob to Pharoah—but we know withall his life was infinitely rich and rewarding. We are pilgrims and sojourners on the earth according to the Scriptures. Here we have no continuing habitation.

All are pilgrims on life's dusty way—and the true man's life embraces action and endurance. Your life is fruitful in the ratio in which it is laid out in patient perseverance and noble action.

Happy and wise is he who determines early to acquire poise (which is patient dignity), dogged determination, and quiet courage—all in order to become a compassionate pilgrim—contributing, consoling, enduring, rejoicing, overcoming, winning—every day even though his days be few and abound with much evil. His life is thus a symphony of satisfaction to himself and a multitude of benefit and blessing to his fellow pilgrims near.

> I expect to pass through this world but once. Any good thing, therefore, that I can do or any kindness I can show to any fellow human being let me do it now. Let me not defer nor neglect it, for I shall not pass this way again.
>
> —Stephen Grellet

AS I GO ON MY WAY

My life shall touch a dozen lives before this day is done—
Leave countless marks for good or ill ere sets this evening
sun.
Shall fair or foul its imprint prove, on those my life shall hail?
Shall benison my impress be, or shall a blight prevail?

When to the last great reckoning the lives I meet must go,
Shall this wee, fleeting touch of mine have added joy or woe?
Shall He who looks their records o'er—of name and time and
place—
Say "Here a blessed influence came" or "Here is evil's trace"?

From out each point of contact of my life with other lives
Flows ever that which helps the one who for the summit
strives.
The troubled souls encountered—does it sweeten with its
touch,
Or does it more embitter those embittered overmuch?

Does love in every handclasp flow in sympathy's caress?
Do those that I have greeted know a newborn hopefulness?
Are tolerance and charity the keynote of my song
As I go plodding onward with earth's eager, anxious throng?

My life shall touch a million lives in some way ere I go
From this dear world of struggle to the land I do not know.
So this the wish I always wish, the prayer I ever pray:
Let my life help the other lives it touches by the way.

—*Strickland Gillilan*

Getting Along

Learning to get along with others is one of the first essentials of living. We spend too little time and thought on this. We don't learn how to deal successfully with the people who are an essential part of our everyday world.

We may say we don't care, but this is hardly true. We might just as well say that we don't want to have friends or that we don't want to be successful or happy.

If you work in an office, merchandising firm, or in any institution with other people, you need to get along with them. If you don't show promise in this, you may not be hired in the first place. Or if you get the job and you can't get along with others in the organization, you may soon lose your job.

Before you join an organization, you should learn to get along with other people. Before you think seriously about selling anything, you should know your ability to deal with others in a pleasant and effective manner. Before you ask a girl to be your wife, you should know how to get along with her, her relatives, and her friends. Before you accept a proposal of marriage you should first determine whether or not you can get along with the man.

Theodore Roosevelt may be correct in his view of this: "The most important single ingredient in the formula of success is knowing how to get along with people."

BEGIN TODAY

So brief a time we have to stay
Along this dear, familiar way:
It seems to me we should be kind
To those whose lives touch yours and mine.

The hands that serve us every day,
Should we not help them while we may?
They are so kind that none can guess
How soon they'll cease our lives to bless.
The hearts that love us, who may know
How soon the long, long way must go.
Then might we not their faults forgive
And make them happy while they live?

So many faults in life there are
We need not go to seek them far;
But time is short and you and I
Might let the little faults go by.

And seek for what is true and fine
In those whose lives touch yours and mine;
This seems to me the better way
Then why not, friend, begin today.

—*Author Unknown*

BY THE SIDE OF A MAN

I want to walk by the side of a man
Who has suffered and seen and knows,
Who has measured his pace on the battle line
And given and taken the blows.
Who has never whined when the scheme went wrong,
Nor scoffed at the failing plan—
But taken his dose with a heart of trust
And the faith of a gentleman;

Who has parried and struck and sought and given,
And, scarred with a thousand spears—
Can lift his head to the stars of heaven
And isn't ashamed of his tears.
I want to grasp the hand of a man
Who has been through it all and seen,
Who has walked in the dark of an unseen dread
And refused to sag or lean;

Who has bared his breast to the wind of dawn
And thirsted and starved and felt
The sting and the bite of the bitter blasts
That the mouths of the foul have dealt;
Who was tempted and fell and rose again,
And has gone on trusty and true,
With God supreme in his manly heart
And his courage burning anew.

I'd give my all—be it little or great—
To walk by his side today
To stand up there with the man who has known
The bite of the burning fray

Who has gritted his teeth and clenched his fist
And gone on doing his best
Because of the love for his fellowman
And the faith in his manly breast.

I would love to walk with him, hand in hand,
Together journey along
For the man who has fought and struggled and won
Is the man who can make men strong.

—*Author Unknown*

TEAM WORK

It's all very well to have courage and skill
    And it's fine to be counted a star,
But the single deed with its touch of thrill
    Doesn't tell the man you are;
For there's no lone hand in the game we
      play,
    We must work to a bigger scheme,
And the thing that counts in the world
      today
    Is, how do you pull with the team?

They may sound your praise and call you
      great,
    They may single you out for fame,
But you must work with your running mate
    Or you'll never win the game;

Oh, never the work of life is done
  By the man with a selfish dream,
For the battle is lost or the battle is won
  By the spirit of the team.

You may think it fine to be praised for skill,
  But a greater thing to do
Is to set your mind and set your will
  On the goal that's just in view;
It's helping your fellowman to score
  When his chances hopeless seem;
It's forgetting self till the game is o'er
  And fighting for the team.

—Edgar A. Guest

Mender of Hearts

In the little churchyard at Ashurst in Sussex, England, is a simple wooden cross that marks the grave of Michael Fairless (Margaret Fairless Barber), who wrote that immortal, though brief, book, *The Roadmender*. On the cross is her name, the date, August 24, 1901, and the words, "Lo, how I loved Thee."

Few authors have written a single book that has had such widespread appeal. *The Roadmender* was published soon after the author's death and has sold over half a million copies in all editions. Says one commentator: "Only the impenetrable mystery of genius can explain the mysterious personality of Michael Fairless, this young girl who adopted a masculine pseudonym and the guise of a roadmender, and gave to the world not only an immortal classic, but a whole philosophy of refined gold."

I was introduced to this book many years ago by George Matthew Adams, who prized it above all his many thousands of treasures. This lover of fine literature, who introduced so many great books to American readers, introduced *The Roadmender* in his beautiful column, "Today's Talk." I have loved the book so much that I have collected it in every edition I could discover. Many are beautifully illustrated in color, with etchings and photography.

In this charming and highly human book the author has taken the roadmender as a symbol of service on the highway of life. In the introductory chapter of the book, Michael Fairless has this to say: "After all, what do we ask of life, here or indeed hereafter, but to serve, to live, to commune with our fellowmen and with ourselves; and from the lap of earth to look up into the face of God?"

Though this little book relates the story of a roadmender, its reading has inspired thousands upon thousands to a more useful life—and I believe that Michael Fairless has helped to mend many a human heart of its aches and hurts, though she confessed that she was "most gladly in debt to all the world; and to Earth, my mother, for her great beauty."

ROAD MAKERS

We shall not travel by the road we make.
Ere day by day the sound of many feet
Is heard upon the stones that now we break,
We shall but come to where the cross-roads
    meet.

For us the heat by day, the cold by night,
The inch-slow progress and the heavy load,
And death at last to close the long, grim fight
With man and beast and stone: for them—
    the road.

For them the shade of trees that now we
    plant,
The safe, smooth journey and the ultimate
    goal—
Yea, birthright in the land of covenant:
For us day-labor, travail of the soul.

And yet the road is ours, as never theirs;
Is not one thing on us alone bestowed?
For us the master-joy, oh, pioneers—
We shall not travel, but we make the road!

—*V. H. Friedlaender*

Chains

"Your sole contribution to the sum of things is yourself."

—*Crane*

"Stone walls do not a prison make nor iron bars a cage," the poet has so aptly said. Multitudes of men are prisoners within walls, cages, and chains of their own making. Chained and hobbled by weaknesses of fear, failure, doubt, and pessimism they drag through endless days of despairing drudgery as shackled prisoners without hope of parole or pardon.

You are chained by your sins, mistakes, and failures of the past—which fill you with remorse and vain regret. These may be forgiven, overcome, and even be made into stepping-stones to goodness and achievement. When you make a mistake don't look back at it long. Think about the reason for it, and then look forward. Mistakes are lessons of wisdom. The past cannot be changed. The future is yet in your power.

You are changed by harmful habits. Face the truth of the poisonous effect of these devilish pursuits and be done with them.

Fear of failure is the chain which binds so many who would otherwise launch out into a new life or another business endeavor. Remember, not failure, but low aim, is crime. "Our doubts are traitors and make us lose the good we oft might win, by fearing to attempt," said Shakespeare. We fall to rise—are baffled to fight better. Believe that you can—then begin at once.

You are to be pitied indeed if you are a prisoner of pro-crastination—putting things off—having good but unat-tempted intentions.

Hope is here together with plenteous pardon with assur-ance of a new life of freedom from your present bondage—plus new energy and enthusiasm to achieve the full satisfying life to which you are entitled. It's entirely up to you—break those chains—be free!

MR. MEANT-TO has a comrade,
    And his name is Didn't Do;
Have you ever chanced to meet them:
    Did they ever call on you?
These two fellows live together
    In the house of Never-Win,
And I'm told that it is haunted
    By the ghost of Might-Have-Been.

—*Author Unknown*

You cannot run away from a weakness; you must sometime fight it out or perish. And if that be so, why not now, and where you stand?

—*Robert Louis Stevenson*

MYSELF

I have to live with myself, and so
I want to be fit for myself to know,
I want to be able, as days go by,
Always to look myself straight in the eye;
I don't want to stand, with the setting sun,
And hate myself for things I have done.

I don't want to keep on a closet shelf
a lot of secrets about myself,
And fool myself, as I come and go,
Into thinking that nobody else will know
The kind of a man I really am;
I don't want to dress up myself in sham.

I want to go out with my head erect,
I want to deserve all men's respect;
But here in the struggle for fame and pelf
I want to be able to like myself.
I don't want to look at myself and know
That I'm bluster and bluff and empty show.

I can never hide myself from me;
I see what others may never see;
I know what others may never know,
I never can fool myself, and so,
Whatever happens, I want to be
Self-respecting and conscience free.

—*Edgar A. Guest*

Habits

Habit is a fixed series of acts. Do a thing once and tracks are marked. Do a thing twice and a route is mapped. Do a thing thrice and a path is blazed.

Do the right thing over and over again.

From the unconscious wink of the eye to the smooth, unnoticed movements of a million worlds, the law of habit relentlessly rules its course. All life is but a set of habits.

Do the right thing over and over again.

If you are prompt today you will want to be prompt tomorrow. If you are fair once you will surely seek to be fair again. The fight for a thing worthwhile right now cannot help but ease the fight for the thing worthwhile later on. It is the law of habit.

Do the right thing over and over again.

DESTINY

From "Raphael"

We shape ourselves the joy or fear
   Of which the coming life is made,
And fill our future's atmosphere
   With sunshine or with shade.

The tissue of the life to be
   We weave with colors all our own,
And in the field of destiny
   We reap as we have sown.

—John Greenleaf Whittier

IF YOU KEEP BUSY

If you were busy being kind,
Before you knew it you would find
You'd soon forget to think 'twas true
That someone was unkind to you.

If you were busy being glad,
And cheering people who are sad,
Although your heart might ache a bit,
You'd soon forget to notice it.

If you were busy being good,
And doing just the best you could,
You'd not have time to blame some man
Who's doing just the best he can.

If you were busy being true
To what you know you ought to do,
You'd be so busy you'd forget
The blunders of the folks you've met.

If you were busy being right,
You'd find yourself too busy, quite,
To criticize your neighbor long
Because he's busy being wrong.

—*Rebecca Foresman*

Blessed is the man that walketh not in the counsel of the ungodly, nor standeth in the way of sinners, nor sitteth in the seat of the scornful. But his delight is in the law of the Lord; and in his law doth he meditate day and night. And he shall be like a tree planted by the rivers of water, that bringeth forth his fruit in his season; his leaf also shall not wither; and whatsoever he doeth shall prosper.

—Psalm 1:1-3

We sow a thought and reap an act,
We sow an act and reap a habit,
We sow a habit and reap a character,
We sow a character and reap a destiny.

—Thackeray

A habit cannot be tossed out the window; it must be coaxed down the stairs a step at a time.

—Mark Twain

"Could the young but realize how soon they will become . . . walking bundles of habits, they would give more heed to their conduct. . . . Every smallest stroke of virtue or of vice leaves its ever so little scar . . . We are . . . imitators and copiers of our past selves."

—William James

The Undisciplined

According to the commentators, the newspapers, and indeed, any two people who get together—the world is in pretty much of a mess. Of course, each person has his own reason and his own solution. Here is mine.

I think most of our trouble stems from those who are undisciplined, from those people who have never learned self-control and have not the inner balance that makes a man capable of governing himself and capable of giving or obeying orders.

In world affairs we have suffered too much from the undisciplined. A dictator—either of the left or right—is undisciplined because he must have everything his own way and for himself. His regimented followers are undisciplined. They cannot act as men capable of making their own decisions and following their own reasoning to a logical conclusion.

In our own nation we have suffered from the undisciplined—from those who will not live by the laws they themselves make, from those who want power and preferment so much they will resort to trickery, false statements, and chicanery to get their own way.

Is that too strong? Then look first around you. Notice the man in the shop who fawns on his superiors and browbeats those beneath him, who is ever ready to seize the credit for another man's work and to put the blame for his own mistakes on someone else. Notice the woman who gossips about things of which she knows nothing in her avidity to become the center of the stage. Notice the politician who stirs up mob feeling with false accusations.

But the undisciplined are not only what the ultra uncharitable call the "lunatic fringe." They are the people who do not keep their word once pledged and who cannot admit an error. They are those who begrudge praise to another and who instinctively lie themselves out of difficulties. They are the ones so busy planning what they are going to say that they never listen to what people are saying to them.

Sure—you know them all, and can name dozens I've overlooked. They are the people who make the trouble.

The solution? Why, let us just be sure *we* are self-disciplined. All great reforms must begin with the individual and the problem of the undisciplined is no exception.

GOD, GIVE US MEN!

God, give us men! A time like this demands
Strong minds, great hearts, true faith and ready hands;
    Men whom the lust of office does not kill;
Men whom the spoils of office cannot buy;
    Men who possess opinions and a will;
Men who have honor; men who will not lie;
Men who can stand before a demagogue
    And damn his treacherous flatteries without winking!
Tall men, sun-crowned, who live above the fog
    In public duty and in private thinking;
For while the rabble, with their thumb-worn creeds,
Their large professions and their little deeds,
Mingle in selfish strife, lo! Freedom weeps,
Wrong rules the land and waiting Justice sleeps.

—*Josiah Gilbert Holland*

Teenagers

A small percentage of our teenagers, like other age groups, are seriously maladjusted, bad, and antisocial. These few create our main social problems among teenagers.

But the vast majority of teenagers learn well the ways of society and find their place, sooner or later. They eventually grow up into stable and socially responsible persons in all areas of life.

Philo Farnsworth invented television at the age of thirteen. George Westinghouse designed the air brake at fifteen. Bryant wrote his famous poem "Thanatopsis" at seventeen. Mahatma Gandhi, though married at thirteen, became the leader and emancipator of India's millions. Victoria began her reign as Queen of England at sixteen. Dick Button won the Olympic figure skating championship at eighteen. William James Sidis graduated from Harvard at sixteen. These teenagers displayed an unusually high level of performance.

Teenagers are not born antisocial. They make mistakes in learning how to live in their world as individuals and as members of groups. They do their best at this through the wise guidance and understanding of mature adults who are always ready to help them find the best way in their world.

EQUIPMENT

Figure it out for yourself, my lad,
You've all that the greatest of men have had,
Two arms, two hands, two legs, two eyes
And brain to use if you would be wise.

With this equipment they all began,
So start for the top and say, "I can."

Look them over, the wise and great,
They take their food from a common plate,
And similar knives and forks they use,
With similar laces they tie their shoes,
The world considers them brave and smart,
But you've all they had when they made their start.

You can triumph and come to skill,
You can be great if you only will.
You're well equipped for what fight you choose,
You have legs and arms and a brain to sue,
And the man who has risen great deeds to do
Began his life with no more than you.

You are the handicap you must face,
You are the one who must choose your place,
You must say where you want to go,
How much you will study the truth to know.
God has equipped you for life, but He
Lets you decide what you want to be.

Courage must come from the soul within,
The man must furnish the will to win.
So figure it out for yourself, my lad.
You were born with all the great have had,
With your equipment they all began
Get hold of yourself, and say: *"I can."*

—*Edgar A. Guest*

A YOUTH'S PRAYER

To build a life that's clean, upright, secure,
God's temple that will through the years endure;
To walk courageously, steadfast, and sure;
   This is my prayer.
To teach a war-torn world the fruits of peace;
To plead that cruelty and hate must cease,
That earth might see goodwill and love increase;
   This is my prayer.
To dedicate my life, my youth, my all
To Christ, and then in answer to his call,
Be faithful to each task—the large, the small;
   This is my prayer.

—*George W. Wiseman*

Real happiness is cheap enough, yet how dearly we pay for its counterfeit.

—*Hosea Ballow*

Dangers of Youth

It's difficult to imagine Art Linkletter in any other role than the happy, friendly entertainer who for many years has entered millions of homes by way of radio and television.

But Art is very serious as he discusses the death of his daughter, Diane, age twenty, who plunged from the kitchen window of a Hollywood apartment while under the influence of LSD. Linkletter says her fatal plunge was the result of taking "a tiger in her bloodstream."

Linkletter often lectures at colleges on the permissiveness of our society which he feels encourages drug use. "I intend to reemphasize that point. I think my daughter's death is going to be paid for many, many times by the kind of things I can say and get done, using this as an example," he says.

"I've been as good a parent as I could possibly be, I think. We've been a very close family. My wife and I have tried to set a good example. We have tried to keep our children up-to-date on what the dangerous things are, but perhaps we did not bear down as hard as we should have.

". . . Diane, of all the children, was always the most daring. She was the most emotionally up and down. She was either on top of the mountain or in the valley of despair—over trivial things."

Diane became an actress, so her father was not too surprised at reports that she might be going with a group that was experimenting around.

"I brought it out, as I do everything," he explains. "Our lines of communication were open as far as I was concerned. I said, 'Diane, is it true this group has been experimenting with some of the new things?' And she admitted that it was.

"I pointed out the obvious dangers. She agreed, and with consummate skill acted out the part that she would never do it again. Obviously she did it again. Over the months she found she had a tiger in her bloodstream.

"Apparently what finally happened was that she became despondent over a spat with her boyfriend and took a much stronger dose of this poison than she should have. She was worried that she would never come out of it mentally, and this led to her death.

"I want the parents and I want their kids to read about this and be shocked, be frightened at what can happen.

"When somebody like Timothy Leary comes out and justifies it, we have got to jump on him with hobnailed boots. Such people are casting doubt on the authority of people who know how deadly these things can be.

"Those kids I've talked to who use it tell me that when you're on what they call a trip, with a heavy dose of LSD, every one of your faults and shortcomings stand out in stark-naked, unrelieved, unrationalized relief. There is no place to hide.

"We know of a college girl who was fed a sugar cube with heavy LSD at a cocktail party by fraternity guys as a joke, and she didn't even know she had taken it. She didn't know there was anything on the cube. She was just taking a tidbit. This was three years ago, and she is still at U.C.L.A. in a ward, practically a vegetable.

"If I can save a few lives . . ." Linkletter didn't finish the sentence.

The advice of the experts—doctors, judges, police, psychiatrists—is crystal-clear and often-expressed: Drugs are dangerous; drugs can kill. Yet there is little the experts can say that is half so eloquent as the tragic stories of the drug users themselves—the children we are losing.

"Happy twenty-first birthday, Johnny." At least, we hope it's happy. Johnny's strung out on "speed," and most people take him for about thirty-five. He's shooting "meth," now, but he started on pills: "dexies," "bennies." He has to use a little more each day to maintain the "high" and avoid "crashing." It's as though he were a car that's raced its motor continuously for a year. No wonder he looks like he's ready for a 50,000 mile overhaul.

You see, on "speed," you don't eat, you don't sleep, you don't feel you have to pay any attention to your health . . . because you feel so "up" all the time.

So while you're "up" on speed, your body runs down. Johnny raps all the time about how, since he's started "speeding," he's really living. At this rate, he may have lived his life before he reaches twenty-two.

—*National Institute of Mental Health*

Pitfalls

Active opposition awaits the progress of every purposeful, pursuing, persevering person in his life pilgrimage. These adversaries are often known and adknowledged but more often lie in wait, hidden, unknown, or unobserved—let's call them pitfalls.

A pitfall is just that—a person, thing, or condition—which if allowed, endured, or indulged fells you into a deep, dark pit of ineffectiveness, misery, defeat, and possible ruin.

We've seen the wreckage wrought by these assailants: laziness, fear, doubt, arrogance, deceit, debauchery, disillusionment, pride, failure, drunkenness, regret, sorrow. These are some of your fiercer foes who would rob you of safety, satisfaction, and success. Beware of these and all their slinking kin. Fear only to tolerate one or all—fail to give ground to a one.

I challenge you young people to consider ever so carefully this forewarning. You of mature years, check-up seriously. Then eyes-front, forward march—armed with the might of a well-ordered moral life—with faith, courage, honesty, self-control, an educated conscience, and a steel determination to make your own noble contribution to this pilgrimage. You will find the victorious life—your intended life of self-confidence, humility, pity, love, concern, awareness, and a mighty confidence in the Eternal—where pitfalls are transformed into power stations and stepping-stones into victory.

A BAG OF TOOLS

Isn't it strange
That princess and Kings,
And clowns that caper
In sawdust rings,
And common people
Like you and me
Are builders for eternity?

Each is given a bag of tools,
A shapeless mass,
A book of rules;
And each must make—
Ere life is flown—
A stumbling block
Or a steppingstone.

—R. L. Sharpe

THE BRIDGE-BUILDER

An old man going a lone highway
Came at the evening, cold and gray,
To a chasm vast and wide and steep,
With waters rolling cold and deep.
The old man crossed in the twilight dim,
The sullen stream had no fears for him;
But he turned when safe on the other side,
And built a bridge to span the tide.

"Old man," said a fellow pilgrim near,
"You are wasting your strength with building here.
Your journey will end with the ending day,
You never again will pass this way.
You've crossed the chasm, deep and wide,
Why build you this bridge at eventide?"

The builder lifted his old gray head.
"Good friend, in the path I have come," he said,
"There followeth after me today
A youth whose feet must pass this way.
The chasm that was as nought to me
To that fair-haired youth may a pitfall be;
He, too, must cross in the twilight dim—
Good friend, I am building this bridge for him."

—*Will Allen Dromgoole*

Spend your time in nothing which you know must be repented of; in nothing on which you might not pray the blessing of God; in nothing which you could not review with a quiet conscience on your dying bed; in nothing which you might not safely and properly be found doing if death should surprise you in the act.

—*Richard Baxter*

TIME

So the sands of Time that
   slowly flow
 From out my hour glass
Will all too soon have ebbed
    away,
  My life will then be past.
So I must make the most of time
   And drift not with the tide,
For killing time's not
    murder,
   It's more like suicide.

—Author Unknown

JUST A MINUTE

I have only just a minute
Only sixty seconds in it,
Forced upon me, can't refuse it,
Didn't seek it, didn't choose it.
But it's up to me to use it,
I must suffer if I lose it,
Give account if I abuse it,
Just a tiny little minute—
But eternity is in it.

—Author Unknown

GREAT HEART

Where are you going, Great-Heart?
  To fight a fight with all my might,
  For Truth and Justice, God and Right,
  To grace all Life with His fair light.
    Then God go with you, Great-Heart!

Where are you going, Great-Heart?
  To lift To-day above the Past;
  To make to-morrow sure and fast;
  To nail God's colors to the mast.
    Then God go with you, Great-Heart!

Where are you going, Great-Heart?
  To set all burdened peoples free;
  To win for all God's liberty;
  To stablish His Sweet Sovereignty.
    God goeth with you, Great-Heart!

—John Oxenham

None but one can harm you,
None but yourself who is your greatest foe;
He that respects himself is safe from others:
He wears a coat of mail that none can pierce.

—Henry Wadsworth Longfellow

Drop Thy still dews of quietness,
  Till all our strivings cease;
Take from our souls the strain and stress,
And let our ordered lives confess
  The beauty of Thy peace.

—John Greenleaf Whittier

Go Ahead, Be A Square

A wise person said that many years ago the word "square" was one of the most honored and respected words in our vocabulary. A square deal was an honest deal. A square meal, a good and full meal.

It was the square-shooter rather than the sharp-shooter who was admired. When you were financially square you paid all your debts.

What is a square today? He is the fellow who never learned to get away with it—being the one who volunteers when he doesn't have to—who tries to do better than others—who has to be reminded to go home because he is so lost in his work. He is the man who says: "I am my brother's keeper."

Don't be afraid to be a square.

OUR HEROES

Here's a hand to the boy who has courage
　To do what he knows to be right;
When he falls in the way of temptation,
　He has a hard battle to fight.
Who strives against self and his comrades
　Will find a most powerful foe.
All honor to him if he conquers.
　A cheer for the boy who says "No!"

There's many a battle fought daily
　The world knows nothing about;
There's many a brave little soldier

Whose strength puts a legion to rout.
And he who fights sin singlehanded
  Is more of a hero, I say,
Than he who leads soldiers to battle
  And conquers by arms in the fray.

Be steadfast, my boy, when you're tempted,
  To do what you know to be right
Stand firm by the colors of manhood,
  And you will o'ercome in the fight.
"The right," be your battle cry ever
  In waging the warfare of life,
And God, who knows who are the heroes,
  Will give you the strength for the strife.

—Phoebe Cary

EVERY YOUTH

Every youth has a quest to make
  For life is the King's Highway;
A joyous heart is the script we take
  On the road to Everyday.
Every youth has his gift to guard,
  As he fares to a far-off goal
A body pure, and a mind unmarred,
  And the light of a lovely soul.
Every youth has a task of his own
  For the Father has willed it so,
Youth seeks the way, and He alone,
  Can show him the path to go.

Every youth has a lovely Guide,
From the vale to the mountain crest,
For the Unseen Friend who walks beside
Is the Way and the End of the quest.

—*Author Unknown*

OF ANCIENT SHACKLES

I am among those unregenerates
Who do not seek "New Freedom,"
    who enjoy
The ancient shackles of old-fashioned love,
Of faith and duty, and would not destroy
All moorings of the spirit that are old.
I like old-fashioned, peaceful firesides,
The steadfastness old homes and
    gardens knew;
I hold the old belief that love abides,
The old sustaining credences of men
That God must be the nurture of the soul,
That He will lean and listen to a prayer
And watches every man move toward His
    goal.
I am an unemancipated one
Who wears such fetters with a full content;
I see New Freedom's tortured restlessness
And of my bonds am deeply reverent.

—*Adelaide Love*

That Mean Ole Mother of Mine

I had the meanest Mother in the world. While other kids ate candy for breakfast, I had to have cereal, eggs, or toast. When others had cokes and candy for lunch, I had to eat sandwiches. As you can guess, my supper was different than the other kids, also. But, at least, I wasn't alone in my sufferings. My sister and two brothers had the same mean mother I had.

My mother insisted upon knowing where we were at all times. You'd think we were on a chain gang. She had to know who our friends were and what we were doing. She insisted if we said we'd be gone one hour or less .⸳. . not one hour and one minute. I am nearly ashamed to admit it, but she actually struck us. Not once, but each time we did as we pleased. Can you imagine someone actually hitting a child just because he disobeyed? Now you can begin to see how mean she really was.

The worst is yet to come. We had to be in bed by nine each night and up early the next morning. We could not sleep till noon like our friends. So while they slept . . . my mother actually had the nerve to break the child labor law. She made us work. We had to wash the dishes, make beds, learn to cook, and all sorts of cruel things. I believe she laid awake at night thinking up mean things to do to us.

She always insisted upon our telling the whole truth and nothing but the truth even if it killed us . . . and it nearly did.

By the time we were teenagers, she was much wiser and our life became even more unbearable. None of this tooting the horn of a car for us to come running. She embarrassed us to no end by making our dates and friends come to the door to get us. I forgot to mention while my friends were dating at the mature age of twelve and thirteen, my old fashioned mother refused to let me date until age fifteen and sixteen. Fifteen, that is if you dated only to go to a school function. That was twice a year.

My mother was a complete failure as a mother. None of us has ever been arrested for beating his mate. Each of my brothers served his time in the service of this country. Whom do we have to blame for the terrible way we turned out? You're right, our mean mother. Look at all the things we missed. We never got to march in a protest parade, got to take part in a riot, burn draft cards, and a million and one other things our friends did. She forced us to grow up into God-fearing, educated honest adults. Using this as a background, I am trying to raise my three children. I stand a little taller and I am filled with pride when one of my children calls me mean. Because you see, I thank God He gave me the meanest mother in the world.

—Author Unknown

DELINQUENT MOMS AND DADS

We've heard a lot in recent months
   of delinquent boys and girls;
They're scorned, maligned, and called by some
   the worst in the world

But, odd as things may sound to you,
    they're not so awfully bad,
They do quite well in spite
    of their delinquent Mom and Dad.
When Dad holds up his stein of brew
    and blows the foam away,
And son stands by, it would be strange
    if that boy failed to stray,
And Mom, with painted lips and toes;
    she is a sight, you bet,
As she uncorks a bottle, too,
    and lights a cigarette.
Don't be too tough on boys and girls
    who never had a chance;
Who learn at home to curse and drink,
    and soon are taught to dance;
Who learn in cabarets and dives
    things that bring hurt and shame;
Delinquent Moms and Dads are those
    who really are to blame.
Let's fill our jails with Moms and Dads
    and save the teen-age throng.
By placing all the blame, my friend,
    right where it should belong.

—Author Unknown

Character

Character does not come by chance; it is the combined work of God and man. The very origin of the word points to this truth. Its root is the Greek word *charraso*, which, with slight change, we translate "harass." As Edward Everett Hale says: "The great trip-hammer of the mind of God hits us hard, again and again, and with every blow the metal struck changes its luster, its strength, even its image and superscription. Its character comes to it because it is pounded by this tremendous hammer. The more it is beaten the more character it has." As coins from the mint, with image and superscription, clear-cut and strong, are in just proportion to the blows received, so character is strong in proportion to the blows it bears in God's mint.

We often speak of sterling character. Do we ever stop to study the meaning of this figure of speech? It comes from the English pound sterling, coin of the realm. A pound sterling is gold pounded till it shows the image of the reigning sovereign. Thus our vernacular, which is a crystallization of the deeper thoughts of the generations forming it, testifies to the value of character by linking its expression with the coin of the realm, the standard of value. Character is the one thing of intrinsic value in the universe, the only thing we can take with us; all else we must leave at the grave.

Character is like a tree and reputation is like its shadow. The shadow is what we think of it; the tree is the real thing.

—*Abraham Lincoln*

COWARD

You have no enemies, you say?
Alas! my friend, the boast is poor—
He who has mingled in the fray
Of duty, that the brave endure,
Must have made foes! If you have none,
Small is the work that you have done;
You've hit no traitor on the hip;
You've dashed no cup from perjured lip;
You've never turned the wrong to right—
You've been a coward in the fight!

—Charles Mackey

Still as of old
Men by themselves are priced—
For thirty pieces Judas sold
Himself, not Christ.

—Hester H. Cholmondeley

BIGOT

Though you be scholarly, beware
    The bigotry of doubt.
Some people take a strange delight
    In blowing candles out.

—Eleanor Slater

BE TRUE

Thou must be true thyself
    If thou the truth wouldst teach;
Thy soul must overflow if thou
    Another's soul wouldst reach!
It needs the overflow of heart
    To give the lips full speech.

Think truly, and thy thoughts
    Shall the world's famine feed;
Speak truly, and each word of thine
    Shall be a fruitful seed;
Live truly, and thy life shall be
    A great and noble creed.

—Horatius Bonar

CHARACTER

"Fame is vapor;
Popularity is an accident.
Riches take wings and fly.
Those who cheer you today
May curse you and stab you tomorrow.
Then there is only one thing left—
That is: *Character*."

—Horace Greeley

Your Thoughts

Your thoughts are more important to you than to the people about you. They set the direction your life will take. They determine largely your relations with other people. Your thoughts lay the foundations for your attitudes, your spirit, and your behavior patterns.

Pure thoughts will build better habits. Think well of people as a whole, believe in them, and you will do your best to help them to make the best of their lives and to play a better part in the family and community. Think of yourself as important, and you will tend to make your thoughts the constructive power of life.

Thoughts lead to acts. Acts repeated form deep-seated habits of living. And habits continued make you what you are. Your destiny, therefore, is bound up with your thoughts. The ancient Stoic philosopher and Roman emperor Marcus Aurelius spoke correctly, "Our life is what our thoughts make it." If so, why not try to make your life what you want it to be?

Build thee more stately mansions, O my soul,
  As the swift seasons roll!
  Leave thy low-vaulted past!
Let each new temple, nobler than the last,
Shut thee from heaven with a dome more vast,
  Till thou at length art free,
Leaving thine outgrown shell by life's unresting sea!

—Oliver Wendell Holmes

THINKING HAPPINESS

Think of the things that make you happy,
   Not the things that make you sad;
Think of the fine and true in mankind,
   Not its sordid side and bad;
Think of the blessings that surround you,
   Not the ones that are denied;
Think of the virtues of your friendships,
   Not the weak and faulty side;

Think of the gains you've made in business,
   Not the losses you've incurred;
Think of the good of you that's spoken,
   Not some cruel, hostile word;
Think of the days of health and pleasure,
   Not the days of woe and pain;
Think of the days alive with sunshine,
   Not the dismal days of rain;

Think of the hopes that lie before you,
   Not the waste that lies behind;
Think of the treasures you have gathered,
   Not the ones you've failed to find;
Think of the service you may render,
   Not of serving self alone;
Think of the happiness of others,
   And in this you'll find your own!

—*Robert E. Farley*

MY MIND TO ME A KINGDOM IS

Excerpts

My mind to me a kingdom is;
  Such present joys therein I find,
That it excels all other bliss
  That earth affords or grows by kind;
Though much I want which most would have,
Yet still my mind forbids to crave.

I see how plenty surfeits oft,
  And hasty climbers soon do fall;
I see that those which are aloft
  Mishap doth threaten most of all,
They get with toil, they keep with fear;
Such cares my mind could never bear.

Content to live, this is my stay;
  I seek no more than may suffice;
I press to bear no haughty sway;
  Look, what I lack my mind supplies:
Lo, thus I triumph like a king,
Content with that my mind doth bring.

Some have too much, yet still do crave;
  I little have, and seek no more:
They are but poor, though much they have,
  And I am rich with little store:
They poor, I rich; they beg, I give;
They lack, I leave; they pine, I live.

I laugh not at another's loss;
  I grudge not at another's gain;
No worldly wave my mind can toss;
  My state at one doth still remain:
I fear no foe, nor fawn on friend;
I loathe not life, nor dread my end.

My wealth is health and perfect ease;
  My conscience clear my chief defense;
I never seek by bribes to please,
  Nor by desert to give offense.
Thus do I live, thus will I die;
Would all did so as well as I!

—*Edward Dyer*

Challenge

One of the greatest pains to human nature is the pain of a new idea.

Who knows how many millions of people had observed steam emerging from a pan of boiling water without giving it a second thought before a Greek philosopher by the name of Hiero realized that the escaping vapor meant power, with the result that he built the scientific toy known as Hiero's engine. And it then took some two thousand years before other men of thought and vision developed this plaything of Hiero's into a practical and useful machine that could move ships and vehicles as they had never been moved before.

An incredible number of discoveries and inventions, large and small, owe their beginnings to the ability of certain people to see in commonplace occurrences the germ of a new idea. An apple falls from a tree, and an Isaac Newton starts thinking about gravity and gravitation. An inquiring mind notes the manner in which spiders string their webs across the corner of a garden, and the design of a suspension bridge is formulated.

"Chance," said Louis Pasteur, "favors the prepared mind." Such a mind was that of Sir Alexander Fleming who noticed that a culture of bacteria had been accidentally contaminated by a mold. The mold, the scientist reasoned, was doing odd things and deserved to be studied further. And thus was born penicillin.

The twitching of a frog's leg when touched by a knife

started Luigi Galvani thinking along lines that led to the discovery of the electric battery. Oersted's chance placing of a wire conducting an electric current near a magnet ultimately led Faraday to the invention of the dynamo. The principle of the pendulum was revealed by the swinging of a lantern suspended from the dome of a cathedral. A teenager by the name of William Henry Perkin who was trying to make artificial quinine in his little laboratory ended up with a sticky mess—from which he extracted the first aniline dyes. And Roentgen happened to notice that cathode rays penetrated black paper. When he finally figured out why, he had discovered X ray.

So it goes. A flash of genius reexamines and analyzes something nobody ever paid attention to previously, and the world changes. But it takes a Newton, a Fleming, a Galvani—or, maybe, a you or me. . . .

> With doubt and dismay you are smitten
> You think there's no chance for you, son?
> Why, the best books haven't been written,
> The best race hasn't been run,
> The best score hasn't been made yet,
> The best song hasn't been sung,
> The best tune hasn't been played yet;
> Cheer up, for the world is young!

> No chance? Why, the world is just eager
> For things that you ought to create
> Its store of true wealth is still meager,

Its needs are incessant and great;
Don't worry and fret, fainthearted,
The chances have just begun.
For the best jobs haven't been started,
The best work hasn't been done.

—*Berton Braley*

A crowd of troubles passed him by
    As he with courage waited;
He said, "Where do you troubles fly
    When you are thus belated?"
"We go," they say, "to those who mope,
    Who look on life dejected,
Who weakly say 'good-bye' to hope,
    We go where we're expected."

—*Francis J. Allison*

Every morning lean thine arms awhile
Upon the window-sill of heaven
And gaze upon thy Lord,
Then, with the vision in thy heart,
Turn strong to meet thy day.

—*Author unknown*

Keep Friends

It is a great deal easier to make friends than to keep them.

A charming manner, a clever mind, a jovial mood, a generous impulse, and a happy occasion can be cause enough to arouse your interest in a person at first encounter, and you go away saying: "I like that fellow" or "I like that girl."

But the real friend grows on you.

At first you may be indifferent. He may repel you. He may be gruff or reserved or have some odd corners that jag you. Perhaps he's so quiet he seems stupid. Maybe he has radical views that he announces belligerently. Or he may appear cynical, or too prim or loquacious or supercilious or egotistical.

But time tells. You are thrown with him again and again. You may have to work with him or play with him, and by and by you realize that the two of you fit.

You can get along with each other; he does not irritate you. You do not have to be always "holding yourself in" when he's around. You may feel he would do anything for you, but be careful; don't ask him for favors. Just content yourself with the pleasant belief that he would do anything for you.

Don't set traps for him. Don't say, "I will ask him to do so and so, and test his friendship." Whoever tempts a friend is unworthy of friendship.

Don't ask him to go out of his way to accommodate you. Don't presume upon his good nature "No one," says Ed Howe, "has ever done much for me. I may have expected a great deal from friends long ago, but I do not now. I have not only learned that if I expect a great deal of them I will be disappointed, I have learned that I have no right to expect it.

Friends are like a pleasant park where you wish to go; while you may enjoy the flowers, you must not cut them."

You will be much more likely to keep friends if you never try to sell them anything, never have money dealings with them, never advise them in any matter where they may possibly lose money, and in short eliminate the dollar entirely from your dealings with them.

Another pretty sure method of losing friends is to strive to improve them. Take for friends those who suit you just as they are.

FRIENDS

Ain't it fine when things are going
   Topsy-turvy and askew
To discover someone showing
   Good old-fashioned faith in you?

Ain't it good when life seems dreary
   And your hopes about to end,
Just to feel the handclasp cheery
   Of a fine old loyal friend?

Gosh! one fellow to another
   Means a lot from day to day,
Seems we're living for each other
   In a friendly sort of way.

When a smile or cheerful greetin'
   Means so much to fellows sore,
Seems we ought to keep repeatin'
   Smiles an' praises more an' more.

—*Edgar A. Guest*

A FRIEND OR TWO

You do not need a score of men to laugh and sing
    with you;
You can be rich in comradeship with just a friend or
    two.
You do not need a monarch's smile to light your way
    along;
Through weal or woe a friend or two will fill your
    days with song.

So let the many go their way, and let the throng
    pass by;
The crowd is but a fickle thing which hears not when
    you sigh.
The multitude is quick to run in search of favorites
    new,
And all that man can hold for grief is just a friend or two.

When winds of failure start to blow, you'll find
    the throng has gone—
The splendour of a brighter flame will always lure
    them on;
But with the ashes of your dreams, and all you
    hoped to do,
You'll find that all you really need is just a friend
    or two.

You cannot know the multitude, however hard you
    try:
It cannot sit about your hearth; it cannot hear you
    sigh;

It cannot read the heart of you, or know the hurts
  you bear;
Its cheers are all for happy men and not for those
  in care.

So let the throng go on its way and let the crowd
  depart;
But one or two will keep the faith when you are
  sick at heart;
And rich you'll be, and comforted, when grey skies
  hide the blue,
If you can turn and share your grief with just a
  friend or two.

—Author Unknown

Self-Respect

Have you ever heard of Maimonides? He was a Jewish philosopher who, eight centuries ago, was the Albert Schweitzer of his time. He devoted his life to caring for the ⸜unfortunate and grappling with the spiritual problems that have disturbed mankind in all ages. In his *Guide of the Perplexed*, written in Arabic, he evolved the lofty concept of God as a divine being, without matter or form, perfect, all-powerful, and omniscient. "When we try to behold His splendor," he wrote, "our vision is blinded with excessive light. When we attempt to measure His power our knowledge becomes ignorance. When we endeavor to describe His love, our language is but the prattle of little children."

Evil, Maimonides believed, is but the absence of good. Each good deed, however unspectacular, is a contribution to the achievement of God's ultimate purpose—a tiny beam that helps to dissipate the darkness. Thus, he gave significance to the life and action of every person, however insignificant that person may seem to himself.

So, don't sell yourself short; you are somebody. God Himself has extended to you a personal invitation to join His household, to become one of His sons.

Believe you are a somebody, and go forward and act accordingly.

THE WORLD WE MAKE

We make the world in which we live
By what we gather and what we give,
By our daily deeds and the things we say,
By what we keep or we cast away.

We make our world by the beauty we see
In a skylark's song or a lilac tree,
In a butterfly's wing, in the pale moon's rise,
And the wonder that lingers in midnight skies.

We make our world by the life we lead,
By the friends we have, by the books we read,
By the pity we show in the hour of care,
By the loads we lift and the love we share.

We make our world by the goals we pursue,
By the heights we seek and the higher view,
By hopes and dreams that reach the sun
And a will to fight till the heights are won.

What is the place in which we dwell,
A hut or a palace, a heaven or hell
We gather and scatter, we take and we give,
We make our world—and there we live.

—Alfred Grant Walton

This above all: to thine own self be true,
And it must follow, as the night the day,
Thou canst not then be false to any man.

—William Shakespeare

SELF-RESPECT

Rightly or wrongly, I conceive self-respect to be belief in one's own worth—worth to God and worth to man.

It may, of course, abnormally develop until it becomes pride, conceit, or arrogance; or it may be minimized, making a man slack, careless, and shabby in character as in dress.

But we can all echo the prayer of the old Edinburgh weaver, "O God, help me to hold a high opinion of myself."

"The first thing to be done to help a man to moral regeneration," says MacDougall, the great psychologist, "is to restore if possible his self-respect."

—*Leslie D. Weatherhead*

STUBBORN OUNCES

You say the little efforts that I make
Will do no good: they never will prevail
To tip the hovering scale
Where justice hangs in balance.
  I don't think
I ever thought they would.
But I am prejudiced beyond debate
In favor of my right to choose which side
Shall feel the stubborn ounces of my weight.

—*Bonaro W. Overstreet*

A Bill of Duties

We are, as individuals and as a nation, very justly proud of our Bill of Rights. It is, indeed, the cornerstone of our liberty. But once I heard a wise man say that in order to maintain and fulfill the Bill of Rights, we needed to develop a Bill of Duties.

Duty is an old fashioned word—and all the modern sophistries will not wipe it out. This country reached its heights under men who were thoroughly trained in the plain homely virtues of loyalty, honesty, and integrity, and who personally applied them to their community life.

We have wandered far from these copy book sayings, and have accepted our rights as special privileges for which no payment was necessary. We must go back to the Proverbs, to the simple statement of right and wrong.

> Righteousness exalteth a nation; but sin is a reproach to any people.
>
> He that justifieth the wicked and he that condemneth the just, even they both are an abomination to the Lord.
>
> Train up a child in the way he should go; and when he is old, he will not depart from it.
>
> Buy the truth and sell it not; get wisdom and instruction and understanding.
>
> He that hath no rule over his own spirit is like a city that is broken down and without walls.
>
> They that forsake the law, praise the wicked, but such as keep the law contend with them.

Only by setting up a Bill of Duties for ourselves can we observe the spirit as well as the letter of the Bill of Rights.

How well do you know this charter of our liberties? Read it over carefully and turn its clauses into inverse ratio. Free press—free to speak the truth but not free to make false statements. Free assembly—for free and friendly discussion, but not to be used to overthrow the government. Freedom to worship—but not to keep anyone else from worshiping. And so on. Each freedom that is given carries with it its duty or restriction as it affects each man's conduct toward his neighbor.

If we will but adhere conscientiously to a Bill of Duties, we need have no fear of retaining the benefits of our Bill of Rights.

People hardly ever make use of the freedom they have, for example, freedom of thought; instead they demand freedom of speech as a compensation.

—*Sören Kierkegaard*

Patriotism depends as much on mutual suffering as on mutual success. It is by that experience of all fortunes and all feelings that a great national character is created.

—*Benjamin Disraeli*

Ill fares the land, to hastening ills a prey,
Where wealth accumulates, and men decay;
Princes and lords may flourish or may fade;
A breath can make them, as a breath has
    made;
But a bold peasantry, their country's pride,
When once destroy'd, can never be supplied.

—Oliver Goldsmith

Governments exist to protect the rights of minorities. The loved and the rich need no protection—they have many friends and few enemies.

—Wendell Phillips

Gold is good in its place, but living, brave, patriotic men are better than gold.

—Abraham Lincoln

Where law ends tyranny begins.

—William Pitt.

Doing Your Thing

It is truly exciting to watch your team putting up a good fight against their opponents while you sit in the bleachers shouting as every fresh score is chalked up on the board. But there is a deeper satisfaction in getting out on the diamond or field or court to take part in the game yourself. The game may be going against you, and you may feel worn out before it is over, but the final whistle brings a pleasure that nothing else can quite replace—the gratification of having had a share in the contest.

The same contrast can be drawn between championship at school and work out in the world. Most students enjoy school—the meeting with classmates and teachers every morning, the assemblies of the student body every week, the lively talk about examinations and promotions at the end of the year. But all the time pupils know that these associations belong to a period of preparation for the activities of mature life.

Glimpses of those activities may be caught almost every day. On his way home in the afternoon a student may stop to watch men at work. Whether these particular activities catch his attention or not, he knows that life is kept going by real work. Occasionally he may look forward to that day when, somewhere among the innumerable occupations of men and women, he will step into a job of his own.

Laborers offer a glimpse of what men strive for in their chosen careers, the difficulties they face without flinching, and the ways in which they work together with their fellows. In addition, the study of the work and careers around us will probably give us a notion of why some men and women are astonishingly successful at their work. In the end we may discover that there is nothing in life more absorbing than choosing and doing a job with heart and soul to the very best of our abilities.

MASTER OF MEN.

"There is a young lad, Master,
With two small fish," they said.
"Five barley loaves he carries, too,
But little use they'd be to you
With thousands wanting bread."

And then the Master saw him,
A slender, growing lad,
Who with impetuous, boyish grace
Turned to His own a wistful face
And offered all he had.

At dusk the lad walked homeward.
What though the stars were dim?
A light within his soul he bore—
He'd not be lonely any more—
The Master needed him.

—Author Unknown

BE TRUE TO YOURSELF

Be true to yourself at the start, young man,
  Be true to yourself and God;
Ere you build your house, mark well the spot,
Test all the ground, and build you not
  On the sand or the shaking sod.

Dig, dig the foundation deep, young man,
  Plant firmly the outer wall;
Let the props be strong and the roof be high,
Like an open turret toward the sky.
  Through which heaven's dews may fall.

Let this be the room of the soul, young man—
  When shadows shall herald care,
A chamber with never a roof or thatch
To hinder the light—or door or latch
  To shut in the spirit's prayer!

Build slow and sure; 'tis for life, young man,
  A life that outlives the breath;
For who shall gainsay the Holy Word?
"Their works do follow them," said the Lord,
  Therein there is no death.

Build deep, and high, and broad, young man,
  As the needful case demands;
Let your title-deeds be clear and bright,
Till you enter your claim to the Lord of Light,
  For the "house not made with hands."

—Author Unknown

Love Is Real

Love as a human emotion is as real as anything in the world. It may be expressed as a feeling of warm personal attachment or deep affection for a friend, parent, child, sweetheart, or things. Or it may be elevated to a reverent affection for God and mankind.

Love in some form is universal. Both the sacred and secular literature of peoples incorporate love in various forms as an essential virtue for all human beings. Its application is a cementing force in groups and an integrating force within the individual person. Love is the great builder, hate the great destroyer.

A biblical writer spoke of love as "stronger than death." A New Testament writer declared, "There is no fear in love; for love casteth out fear," and affirmed, "God is love."

The accumulated folklore of the Western world is filled with such proverbs as these: "Love is the salt of life"; "a penny-weight of love is worth a pound of law"; "Labor is light where love doth pay"; "Hope is the lover's staff"; "Love can make any place agreeable"; "Love conquers all"; and "Spice a dish with love and it pleases every palate."

The eighteenth century critic and poet, Frederic Amiel, a Swiss, spoke with keen insight: "Doubt of the reality of love ends by making us doubt everything."

Love comes unseen; we only see it go.

—*Austin Dobson*

Loving means to love that which is unlovable, or it is no virtue at all; *forgiving* means to pardon the unpardonable, or it is no virtue at all; faith means believing the unbelievable, or it is no virtue at all. And to hope means hoping when things are hopeless, or it is no virtue at all.

—*G. K. Chesterton*

A life without love in it is like a heap of ashes upon a deserted hearth—with the fire dead, the laughter stilled, and the light extinguished. It is like a winter landscape—with the sun hidden, the flowers frozen, and the wind whispering through the withered leaves. God knows we need all the unselfish love that can come to us. For love is seldom unselfish. There is usually the motive and the price.

—*Frank P. Tebbetts*

LOVE'S STRENGTH

Measure thy life by loss instead of gain,
Not by the wine drunk, but the wine poured forth;
For love's strength standeth in love's sacrifice,
And whoso suffers must hath most to give.
For labor, the common lot of man,
Is part of the kind Creator's plan;

And he is a king whose brow is wet
With the pearl-gemmed crown of honest sweat.
Some glorious day, this understood,
All toilers will be a brotherhood,
With brain or hand the purpose is one,
And the Master-workman, God's own Son.

—Author Unknown

Come, let us make love deathless, thou and I,
Seeing that our footing on earth is brief. . . .

—Herbert Trench

A MAN TO KNOW

"He is a man to know,"
They said;
But what there was
That drew them to him
None could clearly tell.
Some said it was his common sense,
While others praised his wit;
Still others claimed his personality was
   great,
But when I talked with him,
I knew it was because
  He liked me very much.

—Doxsee

BECAUSE YOU LOVE ME

Because you love me, I have found
  New joys that were not mine before;
New stars have lightened up my sky
  With glories growing more and more.
Because you love me I can rise
  To the heights of fame and realms
    of power;
Because you love me I may learn
  The highest use of every hour.

Because you love me I can choose
  To look through your dear eyes and
    see
Beyond the beauty of the Now
  Far onward to Eternity.

Because you love me I can wait
  With perfect patience well possessed;
Because you love me all my life
  Is circled with unquestioned rest;
Yes, even Life and even Death
  Is all unquestioned and all blest.

—Author Unknown

BECAUSE YOU CARE

Because you care, each task will be much lighter,
　　Each burden so much easier to bear;
And each new morning's outlook better, brighter,
　　And each new day more blest, because you care.
Because you care, each joy will seem completer,
　　Each treasure doubly dear and true and rare;
And in my heart I'll always find it sweeter
　　To want the higher things, because you care.

—Frank Crane

Love is friendship set to music.

—Pollock

Sunday

Each year, we celebrate two days whose whole significance proceeds from one Person—Christmas that changed our calendar, dividing history in two, and Easter that illumines man's outlook on the darkest human mystery.

The central event of Easter—said to be the best-attested fact in history—cannot be discussed at length in column. Neither can it be ignored. In recognition, therefore, we quote a graduate of the University of Tarsus, a Roman citizen, a patrician who in his young manhood was militant in public affairs and whose remaining writings are now universally acknowledged as the work of a profound philosophical mind. He was conquered by this Easter faith. As a result, declassed socially and economically, he was reduced to supporting himself by sewing tent cloth. Once when he was sick, a Greek doctor named Lucas attended him. What he told the doctor sent Lucas south to Palestine on a research tour, to which we owe the doctor's beautiful Gospel of St. Luke.

That sick patient, Saul of Tarsus (we know him as St. Paul), had this to say about the Easter theme: he said—"The witnesses of the Resurrection are, first Cephas"—one form of St. Peter's name—(Paul knew Cephas), "then the twelve" (that is, Jesus' immediate company), "then five hundred brethren at once, most of whom are alive at the present time" (this was about twenty-five years later), "then James, then all the apostles. These saw him alive and active after death, in the order I have mentioned. Last of all, I myself saw the risen Christ, last as though I were least, for I had persecuted his friends."

Here, however, our remarks must take lower ground. We

shall speak of the phenomenon we call Sunday. Every Sunday of the year has precisely the same significance as Easter Sunday. Sunday is the weekly testimonial to an event of which Easter is the annual festival. In Jesus' nation, Sabbath was the seventh or last day of the week—that is, our Saturday. His Resurrection is said to have occurred in the early dawn of the day following the Sabbath, or the first day of the week—the day we now call Sunday. His friends and followers—comparatively unimportant people—began to keep that day and that hour and thus our Sunday began. Not that it was Sunday to them; it was a business day. They met before they went to work.

From that small beginning, see what has come. Think of the total fact of Sunday—seven weeks and three days of free time given us every year in Sundays. Why? How do you account for it? Nothing in nature marks the Sunday. Day and night are marked by the sun; the moon marks the month; what in nature marks the week? It is not an essential of human nature. You will not find it in Africa, China, Japan, or India, nor even in Russia now. Sunday is the exclusive possession of peoples that honor the Christ of Easter.

Then see the wonder of Sunday. It exerts a power as silent and invincible as the coming of spring. We live in the greatest industrial nation on earth. You would think that nothing could stop it. Nothing ever has stopped it—night nor winter nor flood. Neither war nor world depression has stopped it. The only force that ever stops it is Sunday. We go along all week, tilling or harvesting; making and distributing prodigious quantities of goods; buying and selling; shops clangorous with machinery; railways running full schedule;

banks open; schools in session; legislatures in debate; millions of people busy with ten thousand varieties of tasks—Monday, Tuesday, Wednesday, Thursday, Friday, Saturday without a halt in the throbbing tempo—and then, Saturday night—suddenly—a great silence. Over the land—surcease. Schools closed; stores shut up; courts and legislatures adjourned; no postmen; railways on reduced schedules; even the farm takes on a Sunday quiet. Stand in the midst of the central roar of an industrial empire and hear Sunday come down upon it Saturday night, silencing what neither war nor the worst world depression ever has silenced—the effect is positively uncanny. Sunday!

Stand off and look at it—seven and a half weeks—almost two months' holiday every year without a penny of loss to anyone and with infinite gain to all. Say that it comes from a few poor people who first met early on the first day of the week in honor of the event we celebrate at Easter. Say it comes from One who Himself made the first day of the week forever memorable. In any case, after nineteen centuries, Sunday itself is a tremendous social and economic fact, firmly imbedded in our life, recognized by our laws, possessed by our people. Something of reality must have occurred on that day to have marked it so deeply on the centuries.

A world without a *Sabbath* would be like a man without a smile, like a summer without flowers, and like a homestead without a garden. It is the joyous day of the whole week.

—Beecher

In the end of the sabbath, as it began to dawn toward the first day of the week [that is, Sunday], came Mary Magdalene and the other Mary to see the sepulchre. And, behold, there was a great earthquake: for the angel of the Lord descended from heaven, and came and rolled back the stone from the door, and sat upon it. . . . And the angel answered and said unto the women, Fear not ye: for I know that you seek Jesus, which was crucified. He is not here: for he is risen. . . .

—*Matthew 28:1–6*

Sunday is the golden clasp that binds together the volume of the week.

—*Henry Wadsworth Longfellow*

My Pastor's Pastor

It dawned on me the other day that my pastor has no pastor, no human undershepherd to whom he can turn when the days are dark.

Like most church members, I have called my pastor when there was need; and he has never failed me. But who is his pastor? Who rushes to his side when the load is heavier than he can bear alone?

Is there not something within all of us that cries out for human sympathy and understanding? Is my pastor an exception merely because he is my pastor?

The Savior turned aside to talk with the Father and spent long hours with Him who meets His servants in the secret places, and who never forsakes them. But our Lord also needed John and Peter and James and the others. No doubt in later years those very disciples were grieved because they slept while He suffered alone in the Garden.

I have made a resolution which, by God's help, I shall not break. I am determined that my pastor shall know that I love him and that he shall not lack the sympathetic understanding I can give. As a member of my church I shall, in some way, be the shepherd's friend.

MY PREACHER

Give me the priest these graces shall possess;
Of an ambassador the just address.
A Father's tenderness, a Shepherd's care,

A Leader's courage, which the cross can bear,
A Ruler's arm, a Watchman's wakeful eye,
A Pilot's skill, the helm in storms to ply,
A Fisher's patience, and a Laborer's toil,
A Guide's dexterity to disembroil,
A Prophet's inspiration from above,
A Teacher's knowledge, and a Saviour's love.
Give me a priest, a light upon a hill,
Whose rays his whole circumference can fill,
In God's own Word and Sacred Learning verse,
Deep in the study of the heart immersed,
Who in such souls can the disease descry,
And wisely fair restoratives supply.

—*Thomas Ken*

"IF"

If you can go to church, when all about you,
Are going everywhere but to the house of prayer,
If you can travel straight, when others wobble,
And do not seem to have a righteous care;
If you can undertake a noble service,
Expecting others to pitch in and boost,
But find them doing everything to hinder
Or sitting down like biddies on a roost.

If you possess yourself and pray, "God bless you"
When every muscle in you aches to smite;
When something says, "Give up, give up the struggle
Since others fall, why stand alone, and fight?"
You'll find a Presence by you in the furnace,
You'll find a Presence by you, on the sea,
You'll find a Presence by you, in the battle—
Yes! everywhere and always, Victory!

If you can trust, when others faint and falter,
Or stand and serve, when others flee away,
Unmoved by either Jezebel or Ahab,
Remaining faithful every livelong day,
If you can keep your courage up, and boost it,
Yes! boost the Church right on, until the end,
You'll prove yourself a very Noble Human,
And what is more, you'll be a SAINT, my FRIEND!

—Author Unknown

Being Alone

Learn to be alone.

To be healthily alone is to be morally afire. In such solitude are the ideas of centuries hatched. Big minds think, decide, stand, and conquer, while alone. They self-examine and self-construct.

Learn to think alone.

Lincoln was alone with his pine knots and borrowed books; Hugo was alone with his mean garret and pen; Cromwell was alone at St. Ives behind his plow handle. Wherever great problems or vital decisions have had to be met, men have calmly withdrawn that they might better weigh everything—alone.

Learn to decide alone.

Emerson says—"Trust thyself; every heart vibrates to that iron string." Can a man trust himself away from himself? Is not the vital test and final greatness of a man all focused on his ability to stand absolutely alone in emergencies? Props irritate and unnerve. So do irresponsive natures. The crowd eats away at independence. Real worth tops like a mountain cap. Nobody can mistake it. Like the mountain itself it stands alone. No one will ever do for you what you are able to do for yourself. Alone.

Learn to stand alone.

OUT IN THE FIELDS WITH GOD

The little cares that fretted me
  I lost them yesterday
Among the fields above the sea,
  Among the winds at play;
Among the lowing of the herds,
  The rustling of the trees,
Among the singing of the birds,
  The humming of the bees.
The foolish fears of what might happen
  I cast them all away
Among the clover-scented grass,
  Among the new-mown hay,
Among the husking of the corn,
  Where drowsy posies nod,
Where ill thoughts die and good are born—
  Out in the fields with God.

—Author Unknown

It takes solitude, under the stars, for us to be reminded of our eternal origin and our far destiny.

—Archibald Rutledge

I love to be alone. I never found the companion that was so companionable as solitude.

—Henry David Thoreau

SANCTUARY

'Mid all the traffic of the ways,—
Turmoils without, within,—
Make in my heart a quiet place,
And come and dwell therein!

—A little shrine of quietness,
All sacred to Thyself,
Where Thou shalt all my soul possess
And I may find myself;

—A little shelter from Life's stress,
Where I may lay me prone,
And bare my soul in lowliness,
And know as I am known;

—A solitude where I can think,
A haven of retreat,
Where of Thy Red Wine I may drink
And of Thy White Bread eat;

—A little silent sacred place,
Where we may commune hold;
Where Thy White Love shall me embrace
And from the world enfold;

—A little place of mystic grace,
Of self and sin swept bare,
Where I may look into Thy face,
And talk with Thee in prayer.

Come!—occupy my silent place,
And make Thy dwelling there!
More grace is wrought in quietness
Than any is aware.

—*John Oxenham*

Far Horizons

Where does your skyline end? Abram sat in his tent with the flap down. He was shrouded in gloom. He was tented in despair. His world was small, and he was saying to himself: "Life has been a failure. I was born to found a nation, but old age is on me, and my dream is gone. I am childless, and hope is dead, and the future offers but the grave."

Then God invaded the gloom. He threw back the flap of the old man's tent and said: "Abram, come outside and look toward heaven. Dream again!" And he did, and his manhood returned. He saw the stars. He saw that the world was bigger than the patch of ground on which his tent was pitched. He saw that the sky was higher than his ridgepole. He got a sense of far horizons. His soul revived, and turning his back on the grave, the old man went away to found a nation.

One's horizon is his skyline. It is the boundary of his world, the outer rim of his universe. Some men have a short horizon. They live for the day, for the gratification of the passing moment. They measure things by what is nearest. It is a poor way to live. It shortens everything. It deadens existence. It shrouds us in gloom, and tempts us to despair. We need a sense of far horizons.

Have you climbed a road that was long and toilsome, leading out of flat country to a mountaintop? The road wound and wound, and for a long time there were no vistas. The hill in front of you seemed the end of the world. The barriers about you hedged and oppressed you. Then suddenly you reached a crest, and the world broke away across green fields and hazy ridges and majestic peaks in the distance. You had a vision of far horizons and your soul leaped at the sight.

Man needs a perspective. He needs to get himself and his work in a right relationship to God and his world. One reason we get so quickly discouraged and are so easily defeated is that we have lost our outlook.

Man needs far horizons to steady his convictions. The trouble is, people get short-circuited and go to pieces in a moral crisis. The opinions of the crowd tap them, and they surrender. What they need is to live in contact with the currents from God's throne. God's far horizon is the infinite!

JUSTIFIED

"A man must live!" We justify
Low shift and trick to treason high,
 A little vote for a little gold
 To a whole senate bought and sold,
With this self-evident reply.

But is it so? Pray tell me why
Life at such cost you have to buy?
 In what religion were you told
 "A man must live?"

Imagine for a battle cry
 From soldiers with a sword to hold,
 From soldiers with the flag unrolled,
The coward's whine, this liar's lie,
 "A man must live!"

—*Author Unknown*

Beyond the Farthest Horizon

We have dreamed dreams beyond our comprehending,
Visions too beautiful to be untrue;
We have seen mysteries that yield no clue,
And sought our goals on ways that have no ending.

We have seen loveliness that shall not pass;
We have beheld immortal destinies;

Ay, we whose flesh shall perish as the grass
Have flung the passion of the heart that dies
Into the hope of everlasting life.

But low! remains the miracle supreme,
That we, whom death and change have shown our fate,
We, the chance progeny of earth and time,
Should ask for more than earth and time create,
And, goalless and without the strength to climb,
Should dare to climb where we were born to grope;
That we the lowly could conceive the great,
Dream in our dust of destinies sublime,
And link our moments to immortal hope.
So, let us turn to the unfinished task
That earth demands, strive for one hour to keep
A watch with God, nor watching fall asleep,
Before immortal destinies we ask.
Before we seek to share
A larger purpose, a sublimer care,
Let us o'ercome the bondage of our fears,
And fit ourselves to bear
The burden of our few and sinful years.

Ere we would claim a right to comprehend
The meaning of the life that has no end
Let us be faithful to our passing hours,
And read their beauty, and that light pursue
Which gives the dawn its rose, the noon its blue,
And tells its secret to the wayside flowers.

—*Sidney Royse Lysaght*

Music

Let me go where'er I will
I hear a sky-born music still:
It sounds from all things old,
It sounds from all things young,
From all that's fair, from all that's foul,
Peals out a cheerful song.

It is not only in the rose,
It is not only in the bird,
Not only where the rainbow glows,
Nor in the song of woman heard,
But in the darkest, meanest things
There alway, alway something sings.

'Tis not in the high stars alone,
Nor in the cup of budding flowers,
Nor in the red-breast's mellow tone,
Nor in the bow that smiles in showers,
But in the mud and scum of things
There alway, alway something sings.

—*Ralph Waldo Emerson*

Our lives are songs; God writes the words
And we set them to music at pleasure;
And the song grows glad, or sweet or sad,
As we choose to fashion the measure.

—*Ella Wheeler Wilcox*

Life has loveliness to sell,
   All beautiful and splendid things,
Blue waves whitened on a cliff,
   Soaring fire that sways and sings,
And children's faces looking up
Holding wonder like a cup.

Life has loveliness to sell,
   Music like a curve of gold,
Scent of pine trees in the rain,
   Eyes that love you, arms that hold,
And for your spirit's still delight,
Holy thoughts that star the night.

Spend all you have for loveliness,
   Buy it and never count the cost;
For one white singing hour of peace
Count many a year of strife well lost,
And for a breath of ecstasy
Give all you have been, or could be.

—*Sara Teasdale*

To some of us the thought of God is
like a sort of quiet music playing in
the background of the mind.

—*William James*

Make me too brave to lie or be unkind.
Make me too understanding, too, to mind
The little hurts companions give, and
    friends,
The careless hurts that no one quite
    intends.
May I forget
What ought to be forgotten, and recall,
Unfailing, all
That ought to be recalled, each kindly
    thing,
Forgetting what might sting.
To all upon my way,
Day after day,
Let me be joy, be hope! Let my life sing!

—*Mary Carolyn Davies*

In later life, when we have reached the introspective age and are prone to live in memories rather than in hopes and anticipations, association adds its mystic spell to the charm and potency of certain strains of music. The half-forgotten fragment of a line, heard or recalled by accident, is fraught with recollections sadly sweet, like flowers from the grave of dead joys. It will unlock storehouses of memory.

—*Robert Love Taylor*

And he alone is great who turns the voice of the wind into a song made sweeter by his own loving.

—*Kahlil Gibran*